This book belongs to

English - Swedish

duck   Date _____

Anka

duck

Anka

duck

duck

duck

duck

duck

Make a sentence

horse Date _____

häst

horse   häst

horse
horse
horse
horse
horse

Make a sentence

mouse   Date _____

Musen

mouse

Musen

mouse

mouse

mouse

mouse

mouse

Make a sentence

wolf   Date _____

Varg

wolf

wolf
wolf
wolf
wolf
wolf

Varg

Make a sentence

panda   Date _____

panda

panda panda

panda
panda
panda
panda
panda

Make a sentence

chicken Date _____

kyckling

chicken

chicken

chicken

chicken

chicken

chicken

kyckling

Make a sentence

dinosaur   Date _____

Dinosaurie

dinosaur

dinosaur

dinosaur

dinosaur

dinosaur

dinosaur

Dinosaurie

Make a sentence

elephant   Date _____

elefant

elephant   elefant

elephant

elephant

elephant

elephant

elephant

Make a sentence

cow   **Date** _____

ko

cow   ko

cow

cow

cow

cow

cow

Make a sentence

butterfly   Date _____

fjäril

butterfly fjäril

butterfly

butterfly

butterfly

butterfly

butterfly

Make a sentence

worm   Date _____

Mask

worm

worm
worm
worm
worm
worm

Mask

Make a sentence

puppy

Date _____

valp

puppy valp

Make a sentence

turtle   Date _____

sköldpadda

turtle · sköldpadda

turtle
turtle
turtle
turtle
turtle

Make a sentence

turkey Date _____

Turkiet

turkey

turkey
turkey
turkey
turkey
turkey

Turkiet

Make a sentence

hippopotamus   Date _____

flodhäst

hippopotamus flodhäst

hippopotamus
hippopotamus
hippopotamus
hippopotamus
hippopotamus

Make a sentence

tiger Date _____

tiger

tiger

tiger

tiger

tiger

tiger

tiger

tiger

Make a sentence

hen   Date _____

Höna

hen   Höna

Make a sentence

alligator Date _____

alligator

alligator

alligator

alligator
alligator
alligator
alligator
alligator

Make a sentence

monkey   Date _____

apa

monkey   apa

Make a sentence

spider Date _____

Spindel

spider

spider
spider
spider
spider
spider

Spindel

Make a sentence

shark　　　　　　　　Date _____

haj

shark

haj

shark
shark
shark
shark
shark

Make a sentence

lion   Date _____

lejon

lion   lejon

Make a sentence

snail Date _____

snigel

snail

snigel

Make a sentence

kangaroo Date _____

känguru

kangaroo   känguru

kangaroo
kangaroo
kangaroo
kangaroo
kangaroo

Make a sentence

fox Date _____

räv

fox   räv

Make a sentence

snake   Date _____

orm

snake   orm

snake
snake
snake
snake
snake

Make a sentence

camel Date _____

kamel

camel	kamel

camel
camel
camel
camel
camel

Make a sentence

octopus   Date _____

bläckfisk

octopus

octopus
octopus
octopus
octopus
octopus

bläckfisk

Make a sentence

rooster   Date _____

Tupp

rooster

Tupp

Make a sentence

kitten						Date _____

kattunge

kitten   kattunge

kitten
kitten
kitten
kitten
kitten

Make a sentence

deer   Date _____

rådjur

deer rådjur

Make a sentence

ant   Date_____

myra

ant

myra

ant

ant

ant

ant

ant

Make a sentence

dog Date _____

hund

dog

hund

Make a sentence

giraffe Date _____

giraff

giraffe

giraffe

giraffe

giraffe

giraffe

giraffe

giraff

Make a sentence

cat   Date _____

katt

cat

katt

Make a sentence

crab Date _____

Krabba

crab

crab
crab
crab
crab
crab

Krabba

Make a sentence

zebra   Date _____

zebra

zebra zebra

zebra
zebra
zebra
zebra
zebra

Make a sentence

eagle   Date _____

Örn

eagle

eagle

eagle

eagle

eagle

eagle

Örn

Make a sentence

rabbit Date _____

kanin

rabbit

rabbit

rabbit

rabbit

rabbit

rabbit

kanin

Make a sentence

sheep   Date_____

får

sheep   får

Make a sentence

fish   Date_____

fisk   

fish   fisk

Make a sentence

bird Date _____

fågel

bird

fågel

bird
bird
bird
bird
bird

Make a sentence

dolphin   Date _____

delfin

dolphin

delfin

dolphin
dolphin
dolphin
dolphin
dolphin

Make a sentence

bee   Date _____

bi   

bee

bi

Make a sentence

hedgehog   Date _____

Igelkott

hedgehog

hedgehog

hedgehog

hedgehog

hedgehog

hedgehog

Igelkott

Make a sentence

lobster Date _____

hummer

lobster   hummer

Make a sentence

owl Date_____

Uggla

owl
Uggla

owl
owl
owl
owl
owl

Make a sentence

frog   Date_____

groda

frog groda

frog
frog
frog
frog
frog

Make a sentence

pig Date_____

gris

pig

gris

Make a sentence

goat　　　　　　　Date_____

get　　　

goat

goat
goat
goat
goat
goat

get

Make a sentence

dragonfly Date _____

Dragonfly

dragonfly　　　　Dragonfly

dragonfly
dragonfly
dragonfly
dragonfly
dragonfly

Make a sentence

squirrel   Date_____

ekorre

squirrel

ekorre

Make a sentence

parrot   Date_____

Papegoja

parrot   Papegoja

parrot
parrot
parrot
parrot
parrot

Make a sentence

Made in the USA
Las Vegas, NV
08 May 2022